*Pioneer*MISSION

The travel guide for missional adventurers

Peter J Farmer and Tim Nash

WHO ARE *NEWFORMS*?

Pioneer Mission is part of the *Pioneer Series* published by *Newforms*. It's based on a training system of the same name created and delivered by *Newforms Resources.*

Newforms is a training and resource company that serves church planting movements and the simple organic missional churches they are birthing across Britain and beyond. To achieve this aim, *Newforms* offers consultancy, workshops, courses, seminars and short-term mission experiences and facilitates national and regional gatherings.

To find out more, visit newformsresources.com.

ISBN: 978-1-4475-6149-1

Front cover designed by Etherscape. www.etherscape.co.uk

WHAT IS *PIONEER MISSION* ABOUT?

Pioneer Mission is a travel guide for your missional adventures. It outlines the *Pioneer Process* that Jesus modelled and passed onto his 12 disciples, then to 72 others and finally to his global church throughout history.

We hope to pass onto you what we've learnt on our own pioneer journeys. We'll do this through a series of basic practices that will equip you to form simple, organic, missional communities that meet in homes, cafes, workplaces, schools, youth centres, prisons or even church buildings!

WHO ARE PETER AND TIM?

Peter has been involved in pioneer mission for over 10 years. He's the director of *Newforms*, through which he travels extensively across the 12 regions of Britain, connecting and equipping pioneers and entrepreneurs. He's also the founder of missionbritain.com and helped develop simplechurch.co.uk. He is married to Marsha and has three children. Together they enjoy creativity, travel and watching inspiring films together. Peter blogs at peterjfarmer.com.

Tim studied theology at Birmingham Christian College and went on to work as Bible Society's Corporate Researcher. He then studied for a Masters in theology at London School of Theology and is currently employed by the Methodist Church as a pioneer worker among young adults. Tim is married to Hannah. Together they like watching DVD box-sets and fixing up old furniture. Tim podcasts at nomadpodcast.co.uk and blogs at nomadblog.co.uk.

TRAVEL ITINERARY

WHAT IS PIONEER MISSION?

Pioneer Mission is a very different journey from 'friendship evangelism'. Friendship evangelism is our day-to-day witness through our existing social networks at home, work and leisure. The trouble with friendship evangelism is that it leaves unreached those people groups who don't already have connections with Christians. They can only be reached through a more pioneering approach.

In Bible times, Jewish social networks, for example, didn't overlap with the Samaritans (to put it politely!). So for the message of God's Kingdom to reach the Samaritans, Jesus had to pioneer a new connection. He hung around a well near a Samaritan town until a woman came to get water. This created an opportunity for Jesus to spend two days sharing his message with the whole town. Once he had established a community of believers, Jesus moved on (Jn. 4:1-42). This is Pioneer Mission.

Pioneers are people who follow God's call into places where his people haven't gone before. You'll find them hanging around rough backstreet pubs or New Age shops or moving into deprived inner-city estates. Pioneers look for an adventure, a challenge, a risk…

AM I CALLED TO PIONEER MISSION?

We know what you're thinking (because we've thought it, too). You're thinking that you haven't been 'called' to pioneer mission.

It's true that some people have a special God-given 'apostolic' gift that enables them to successfully engage in cross-cultural mission and form new churches. But we also strongly believe that everyone has a general calling to this work.

The Bible clearly says that some people are given a gift of teaching, for example. But it also says that we should all be teaching each other (Col. 3:16). The Bible says that some people have been given a pastoral gift. But it also says that we should all be caring for each other (Gal. 6:2).

Is this a contradiction? Actually, when someone is given a special gift from God it not only means they are enabled to do that work themselves but that they are also called to equip everyone else in this work. Paul the apostle made this clear when he said "It was he who called some to be apostles, some to be prophets, some to be evangelists and some to be pastors and teachers, to prepare God's people for works of service" (Eph. 4:11-12).

So there's no excuse. We're all called to pioneer mission.

WHAT WILL THIS GUIDE HELP ME DO?

It'll help you overcome your boredom
The story of Jesus and the Early Church is a rip-roaring adventure! Every page is packed with demonic encounters, miraculous healings, bust-ups with the religious establishment, fear and doubt, intense excitement and joy. So why does our experience of church often feel so far from this?

Well it's no coincidence that much of the excitement of the early followers of Jesus happened in the context of pioneer mission. Jesus sent his followers to new places to engage with new people (the essence of pioneer mission). And it was there that things happened. Jesus deliberately sent them into situations where he knew they'd be completely out of their depth because then they'd have to rely on God. So we guarantee that if you follow all the suggestions in this guide your faith will never be the same again!

It'll help you form new churches

At the heart of this guide is forming new churches (lower boredom levels is just a nice side effect!). Actually, the heart of the whole process is making disciples, who themselves will make disciples. But we believe the best context for this is through the formation of new churches.

The process is based on seven practices we've drawn from Jesus's own teaching on pioneer mission (which you can find in Matthew 10 and Luke 10). These practices enabled Jesus's followers to form new churches that themselves formed new churches and kicked off a whole movement that changed the world. We firmly believe that these '7 Practices' are as potent today as they were 2,000 years ago. We also believe that if we fully commit ourselves to prayerfully follow these practices our society will be transformed.

WHAT DO I NEED TO KNOW TO GET STARTED?

It's an experiential journey

Travel Guides are designed to be read on the journey. We can't imagine many people discovering the joy of travel by sitting at home reading a guide. Similarly, *Pioneer Mission* hasn't been written to give you information about mission, but rather to accompany you as you experience your own missional journey.

Don't get us wrong, we know information is important. But we believe the Bible challenges our traditional Western understanding of how we relate to it.

'Knowledge' in the Bible doesn't refer to simply acquiring information. The Bible doesn't seem particularly interested in information 'about' something. Instead, knowledge is something much more experiential. So, for example, Adam 'knew' Eve and as a result she conceived Cain (Gen. 4:1 NKJV). Clearly Eve didn't get pregnant because Adam understood certain facts about her! Instead, Adam came to know his wife on the most physical, experiential and intimate level.

According to the Bible, to really *know* something is to act on it, to experience it, to live it. It's this understanding of knowledge that underlies this guide. It isn't enough to simply look up the verses and talk about them. You'll only really *know* what pioneer mission is when you start out on the journey.

To remind us of this, we like to talk about 'Truth+Dare'. We read the truth in the Bible and then we dare each other to get out there and do it!

It's a shared journey
In our opinion, you get the most out of travel when you share the journey. So we believe you'll get the most out of this missional journey if you experience it in community.

Christianity is a communal faith. When Jesus taught us to pray, he didn't tell us to say 'My father in heaven', 'Give me today my daily bread', 'forgive me my debts' and 'lead me not into temptation' (Mt. 4:9-13). Instead, the prayer Jesus taught us was a communal one. In the same way, Jesus assumed that we would be undertaking pioneer mission with a group. So when Jesus taught the principles of pioneer mission, he did so to a group of 12 and a group of 72 (Mt. 10; Lk. 10). Then when he sent them out for practical experience, he told them to go in twos. So we'd strongly encourage you to start out this journey in a group (of somewhere between 2 and 72 people!).

It's an evolving journey

We'd encourage you to treat this guide as a companion on your pioneer mission journey. Rather than a traditional study guide where you move in a linear fashion through the various weeks of study, we'd encourage you to be sensitive to what the Spirit is doing in your group. So, for example, you may feel it's right to dwell on the first topic of 'Pray' for two or three weeks until your vision begins to form. When this vision takes shape, you may feel you don't need to spend very long on the second phase of 'People and Places' because you already have the detail you need. Or later on in the course, you may want to return to 'Pray' to refocus your vision.

So please treat this guide as a flexible resource that you can adapt as your group moves forward on its own unique journey. Our hope is that by the end of this journey your *Pioneer Mission* guide will look like all good travel guides: dog-eared, full of notes and covered in coffee stains!

It's a journey that requires a tour guide

Jesus's disciple Thomas wanted to know the way to the Father's house and was hoping Jesus would give him some directions. Jesus simply responded, 'I am the way' (Jn. 14:1-5). It seems almost too obvious to have to state that Jesus is our guide. But we've found that the reality of this is easily forgotten when we're formulating a strategy for mission. We need to seek Jesus at every step.

Time and again we've set out with a particular strategy in mind, but as we've prayed Jesus opened up a new opportunity that just wasn't on our radar. Jesus said that his Spirit is going through the world testifying to him and persuading people to respond (Jn. 15:26-27; 16:5-11). Our primary task in mission is to be sensitive to what the Spirit of Jesus is doing and join him.

With Jesus as our tour guide, we don't believe this journey needs a human guide. Having said that, we *do* think you'll find it helpful to appoint someone to facilitate your group gatherings. So, for example, it would be helpful for someone to read out this introductory information to the group. That person can also help the discussions flow by asking some of the questions we suggest and perhaps feeding into the discussion some of our understandings and experience. This needs to be a low-profile role though. Remember that the delegated person is an encourager and facilitator, not a leader.

HOW DO I GET STARTED?

This workbook outlines what we call the *Pioneer Process*. This process is made up of 7 Practices (all conveniently beginning with the letter 'P'!) we've drawn from Jesus's teaching on pioneer mission. We'll leave it up to you to decide how many weeks your group journeys through this process, but we'd advice you not to cover more than two practices in one gathering.

We'll briefly outline the 7 Practices now to help you understand the flow of the travel guide, what the learning objectives are and what preparations you may need to make.

Practice 1: Pray

Objective: Prayer is the heartbeat of pioneer mission, so this first session will be the longest and most detailed. The session aims to encourage commitment to various prayer practices that will help us discern the mission God is calling us to.

Preparation: The session will end by praying for each other to be filled with the Spirit. Think about how you could facilitate this in a creative and engaging way (e.g. candles, oil to anoint each other, music, etc.).

Practice 2: People and Places

Objective: This session will get us started with some basic research into the people and places God is calling us to. This will enable us to determine the best ways to make new connections with people.

Preparation: We'll be starting the research during this session. To help the group get started on this, bring along to the gathering some local newspapers, a recording of the local TV news and a laptop. You might also find it helpful to have a flipchart and pens. Also, be prepared to end the evening by going to a public venue in the area you feel called to.

Practice 3: Preach

Objective: This session will focus on how we begin to spread the message of God's Kingdom among the people we feel called to.

Preparation: The session will involve commissioning each other to the work God has called us to. This will involve fasting together, so make sure the group is reminded of this. We suggest you end the fast during this session with a bring-and-share meal.

Practice 4: Power

Objective: This session will look at how we demonstrate the reality of God's Kingdom with the Spirit's power.

Preparation: The session will include an opportunity to pray for healing and deliverance, so you may want to bring some anointing oil.

Practice 5: Person of Peace

Objective: This session will look at the connections we hope to make with key people within a particular place or group of people. It's through these people the message will spread, giving birth to new churches.

Preparation: The group should only move onto this practice when they have started making good connections and are 'preaching' in the places or among the people God has called them to.

Practice 6: Plant

Objective: 'Planting' refers to the process that leads to the formation of new Jesus-centred communities. This session will look at how these communities are formed in such a way that they can function simply and multiply.

Preparation: The session will involve praying for a refilling of the Spirit. You may want to symbolise this in some way, perhaps by lighting a candle or anointing with oil.

Practice 7: Persecution

Objective: This practice looks at how to stand firm against the spiritual and human opposition that inevitably comes when we step out in pioneer mission.

We'll engage with the 7 Practices by Praying to Jesus, Reporting back, Engaging with his word and then Practicing the truth (or PREPing for mission!).

Then at the end of each practice we'll briefly share one or two of our own stories to help show how this theory has proved effective in our experience.

That's everything you need to know about this course. So it's now time to gather a small group of potential fellow Pioneers and begin your missional adventure.

PRACTICE 1: *PRAY*
[Matthew 10:1-5]

PRACTICE 1: PRAY

It's hard to overstate the importance of prayer in pioneer mission, so consequently we'll be going into more detail on this practice than the other six. We suggest you spend at least one whole session looking at prayer, but it's likely that you'll need more than this.

Your group can only really set out on this pioneer journey when you've begun to hear God calling you to a particular people or place. This calling could be to a town or village, a particular housing estate, a local pub or club, New Agers, the unemployed or any number of other possibilities. It may be you've had prophetic words in the past or are already acting on the passions God has given you and have been repeatedly drawn to particular places or people groups. In whatever way God speaks to you, it's important that your group hears his specific call.

Pray
Start with prayer, committing this new journey to God.

It's not uncommon for people to feel they 'ought' to do mission. While mission is a responsibility we need to take seriously, we shouldn't be motivated solely by a sense of duty. God sent Jesus because he 'loved the world' (Jn. 3:16). And Jesus willingly obeyed because he loved us (Jn. 15:13). Love should be our motivation. Spend time praying that as God reveals the people and places he's calling us to, he will also give us a deeper love for them.

Report back
Jesus taught his followers the Pioneer Process and sent them out on mission. When they returned, they reported on what

they'd done and said — before Jesus gave them any further instruction (Lk. 10:17-20).

Although we haven't yet begun the Pioneer Process together, we can still spend some time reporting back on our previous mission experiences.

- *What previous experiences of mission have you had?*

    ....

    ....

    ....

- *What were the particular joys and challenges?*

    ....

    ....

    ....

Engage

Ask someone in the group to read Matthew 10:1-5 out loud.

You may find it helpful to read it a couple of times in different translations.

We'd encourage you at this point to facilitate a time of individual meditation on Jesus's teaching. Spend 5-10 minutes quietly and slowly reading and re-reading the passage. Try and be sensitive to any words, phrases, ideas or questions the Spirit brings to your attention.

- *What is Jesus saying to you about pioneer mission and what does he want you to do about it?*

....

....

....

After this period of individual meditation, spend some time as a group sharing what Jesus revealed to you. You can ask some of the following questions if you feel the discussion needs some direction.

- *Who initiates pioneer mission?*

....

....

....

- *How might we expect this call to mission to happen?*

....

....

....

- *Where does our authority for mission come from?*

....

....

....

- *What other authorities might be challenged by this?*

  ....
  ....
  ....

- *What are we given power for?*

  ....
  ....
  ....

- *Have you ever had any experience of this power?*

  ....
  ....
  ....

- *How would you feel about being given this sort of power?*

  ....
  ....
  ....

- *What responsibilities come with this sort of power?*

  ....
  ....
  ....

- *Who guides our ongoing mission?*

....

....

....

- *How might this guidance come?*

....

....

....

Practice

Your discussion of Matthew 10:1-5 should have centred on Jesus. It's clear from the passage that he's the one who initiates mission and gives us authority, power and ongoing guidance. The question is: how do we put this into practice? The simple answer is, of course, we pray. But there are a number of different ways we can go about prayer that will enable us to hear Jesus's voice more clearly.

1. Listening practices for mission

We're not encouraging the same level of discussion during this stage of the session. Instead, encourage the group to commit to trying out these practices. Then over the following weeks they can discuss their experiences of them. So for now, simply describe these practices to the group and ask how they might go about building them into their lives.

Solitude

Solitude was one of Jesus's most important prayer practices. Time and again the gospels describe Jesus withdrawing to 'lonely places' to pray and seek direction for his mission (Lk. 5:16). Jesus instructed his followers to observe this practice of solitude, encouraging them, for example, to go to their rooms, close the door and pray quietly (Mt. 6:6). While this clearly implies personal prayer, we believe it's also important we experience solitude as a group. Jesus, for example, often withdrew with his disciples (Mk. 3:7).

The reason for solitude is obvious. We're physically removing ourselves from distractions in order to listen to God.

- *How might your group withdraw in order to focus more fully on hearing God's voice?*

  ....

  ....

  ....

Meditation

Meditation seems to be somewhat out of favour with Western Christians right now (perhaps in reaction to its popularity among New Agers). But meditation is a vital part of Christian spirituality and can be found throughout the Bible (just read Psalm 119, for example).

There's a fundamental difference between Christian meditation and eastern forms of meditation. As Christians, we aren't seeking to empty our minds, but rather to fill our minds with God. We can do this by simply sitting silently in God's presence, or by reflecting on his word or on his creation. As we do this, we need to stay conscious of what God might be trying to communicate to us. In our experience, this often comes in the form of unexpected and spontaneous thoughts and ideas. It's important, however, that we check these thoughts with other Christians and against God's word.

- *How will you build meditation into your prayer life?*

....

....

....

Journaling

Journaling is a practice we've found invaluable in the pioneer mission process. As well as being a useful tool for organising your thoughts and as a reminder of what God has done through us, it can also help us hear God's voice.

Some Christians find it hard to hear God's voice when simply sitting passively. We ask God a question but often fail to listen carefully for an answer. Journaling allows us to more actively engage with God. This practice simply involves writing down a question to God (for example, 'which people group are you calling me to?') and then prayerfully writing a response. It often seems that the act of beginning to write gives God permission to shape our thoughts and guide our writing. Read Habakkuk, for example, which is a series of written questions to God and responses from him.

This practice isn't to be confused with the occult practice of 'automatic writing' where the writer loses physical control of their writing hand. Rather, this is God gently guiding our thoughts as we write, much as he would have done with the apostles as they wrote their letters.

- *How can you build journaling into your prayer life?*

....

....

....

Creative prayer

There's no limit to the creative ways we can engage with God. Creative prayer can involve arts and crafts or actively engaging the imagination in meditation (for example, picturing yourself in the throne room of God as you pray).

As with journaling, creative prayer allows us to more actively engage with God and allows him to shape and speak through the creative gifts he has given us. The Old Testament prophets often creatively communicated God's word to the nation through drama, model making and storytelling.

- *How could your group engage with God more creatively?*

....

....

....

Prayer-walking

Prayer-walking is another way of actively engaging in mission-related prayer. There are a number of occasions in the Bible where God called his followers to walk around the place he was calling them to (e.g. Gen. 13:14-17; Josh. 1:3). This practice allows us to actually *see* the people and places God has called us to and the issues there. This was Paul's experience as he walked the streets of Athens (Acts 17:16).

Indeed, Jesus told his followers to pray as they travelled to and around the places he was sending them (Lk. 10:1-5). So rather than simply sitting at home praying for the place God has called you to, why not actually walk the streets of that place as you pray?

We've found it helpful to be strategic in the way we prayer-walk. So, for example, we'll get a map of the area and mark off each street that we prayer-walk until we've covered the whole area. Or, if the area you're called to is large, then perhaps walk the key centres or boundaries.

- *What would be the best way to organise prayer-walking with your group?*

....

....

....

Night prayer
Praying through the night was another important prayer practice of Jesus. Before Jesus chose his pioneer mission team he spent the night in prayer (Luke 6:12-13).

Night prayer doesn't necessarily mean praying through the entire night (although this is what Jesus did on many occasions). There is evidence in the New Testament that the night was divided up into four watches: 6-9pm, 9pm-12am, 12-3am and 3-6am. So praying through one or two of these watches could be a good introduction to night prayer.

- *When could your group get together for night prayer?*

....

....

....

Fasting

Jesus assumed that his followers would regularly fast (Mt. 6:16-18) and saw fasting as a vital weapon in spiritual warfare (Mk. 9:29). So it's no surprise that fasting became an important part of Christian spirituality. We know from historical documents written shortly after New Testament times (e.g. the *Didache* chapter 8) that Christians fasted twice a week.

Apart from the amount of time fasting frees up for prayer, there seems to be a connection between denying our flesh and becoming more spiritually attuned. Fasting says that God is the source and sustainer of life, not the food we eat.

There are no rules on how to fast. In the Bible, we see people undertaking all sorts of different fasts. Some went without food from anywhere between 1 and 40 days, while others undertook partial fasts. Daniel, for example, fasted from the royal food and only ate vegetables and drank water (Dan. 1:8-16). Paul encouraged the married couples in the Corinthian church to fast from sex to enable them to focus more on prayer (1 Cor. 7:5).

- *What sort of fast could your group undertake?*

....

....

....

2. Equipping practices for mission

Now that we've spent some time looking at the various ways in which we can attune ourselves to God's voice, we will also briefly look at some of the things we need to ask God for in order to be equipped for mission.

Mission opportunities

Paul frequently asked his co-workers and partner churches to pray for opportunities for him to proclaim the gospel (Col. 4:2-4). This would naturally also involve asking God to lead you to the 'Person of Peace' (which we'll look at in a later session). Praying for opportunities in mission and for God to make clear where he's calling us to needs to be at the heart of our requests to God.

- *Stop and pray right now that God will reveal to the group where or who he is calling you to and that he will 'open doors' for effective work.*

Mission team

Jesus told his followers that they must pray for more workers as the harvest is so big (Lk. 10:2). So as well as praying for opportunities for mission, we also need to pray that God will send more workers to join us. We've found it helpful to set our alarms every day at 10:02 to remind us to pray for God to send more workers (e.g. Lk.10:2).

- *Set the alarms on your phones or watches now to chime every day at 10:02.*

Mission warfare

Paul made it clear that the struggle we're in is not with humans themselves but with the rebellious spiritual powers that have taken them captive. We're called to love and bless every human we come across and aggressively confront any spiritual power we sense leading them astray (Eph. 6:10-18).

Consequently, we need to make sure we're fully protected. We do this by living in truth, righteousness, peace, faith and salvation. We also need to hone our weapon skills, i.e. our use of God's Word (Eph. 6:14-17).

Spiritual warfare is at the heart of Jesus's mission. He came to defeat the 'prince of this world' (i.e. the devil) (Jn. 14:30). Throughout his ministry, he pushed back the Kingdom of Satan and advanced the Kingdom of God by delivering people from demons and healing them from disease and disability. Jesus likened this activity to 'binding the strongman' and then 'carrying off his possessions' (Mt. 12:29). So as we pray for the people and places Jesus has called us to we can announce that Satan is bound and then carry off his possessions by preaching the gospel and praying for people to be healed and delivered.

- *Stop and pray right now. Announce the arrival of the Kingdom of God, the binding of Satan and the setting free of his captives.*

Mission power
Jesus was clear that the task of pioneer mission shouldn't begin until his team had been filled with the Holy Spirit and had received power (Acts 1:4, 8). It was only when the apostles were filled with the Spirit that they were given the boldness to proclaim God's Kingdom (Acts 4:29-31). Courage is not the absence of fear, but the mastering of it!

Christians aren't always agreed on when this filling takes place or what we should expect when it does take place. We believe, however, that Acts shows that this process of filling is separate from conversion and that we're aware when it has happened (Acts 8:14-17; 19:1-6). We also believe that this isn't a one-off event, but an ongoing process (Eph. 5:18).

- *Spend time right now laying hands on each other and praying to be filled, or refilled, with the Holy Spirit and given power and boldness for mission.*
- *Commit to making this part of the group's ongoing practice.*

Truth+Dare

You're now PREPed in the first practice of pioneer mission! So now you know the truth of the importance of prayer in mission, we dare you to act on it!

- *Which of these practises will you commit to this week?*

....

....

....

- *Will you, for example, set your alarms for the Luke 10:2b Prayer?*

....

....

....

- *Where will you begin to prayer-walk?*

....

....

....

- *How will you build the other practices into the ongoing life of your group?*

....

....

....

Write down specific goals for how each of you will engage with this first practice over the coming week. Be prepared to report back at your next gathering on how you've got on, focusing particularly on where or who you sense God calling the group to. If at your next gathering you still don't have a clear sense of God's call, then we suggest you continue to pray until that call becomes clearer, and only then progress onto the next practice in this guide.

Our Travels

Prayer-walking (Pete)

One of the first things I learned about mission-related prayer was the power of prayer-walking. I began on an inner-city estate over 10 years ago. Each week, I walked a different area. As I walked, I was confronted by all kinds of problems, such as vandalism, drug-dealing and derelict housing.

God's Spirit began to reveal to me the spiritual reality behind these 'human' problems. In response to this revelation, I started praying much more strategically. For example, I began the practice of 'binding the strongman' behind the problems I saw, such as alcoholism, drugs and poverty.

Over the next few years, the area began to change! The council improved the parks, renovated houses and installed security cameras. The atmosphere of the whole area changed. Its physical appearance improved and problems such as the drug dealing began to decrease.

Solitude (Pete)

For a number of years now, I've gone on 3-day retreats every 3 or 4 months to spend time in solitude with Jesus. Sometimes this has simply involved shutting myself away in a room and waiting on Jesus. On other occasions, it has involved extensive study of the Bible on a particular topic I've felt Jesus draw my attention to. At other times, I've felt led to simply walk for hours through the woods. Whenever I have spent these times in solitude, it has always changed me!

For the first day I often feel very restless. It can take me quite a while to become still and focused on Jesus. When the second day comes, I begin to adjust and by the third day I'm beginning to become attuned to God and start to receive revelation from him.

It's during these times of solitude that my vision for the work God is calling me to has enlarged and I've begun to appreciate the bigger picture. It was out of one of these times, for example, that God dramatically broadened my vision and spoke to me about Mission Britain!

Journaling (Tim)

Discovering journaling has profoundly affected my relationship with God and how he's used me in mission. I'd often try to spend time simply being in God's presence, waiting for his guidance, but I always became frustrated by how quickly my mind wandered.

Then God began to reveal to me the art of journaling. He showed me that I could be more actively engaged in prayer by writing out my ideas, concerns and need for guidance. This dramatically increased my ability to focus on God for longer periods of time and gave me a much greater sense of his presence and guidance.

Then God began to show me how to apply this to mission. As I was journaling one day, I sensed God begin to speak to me about a local New Age shop. As I wrote, a message from God to the assistant of this shop began to take shape. Later that week, I was able to pass this message from God on to the assistant. Although she seemed somewhat surprised, she also seemed moved by these words.

Notes, doodles, sketches…

PRACTICE 2: *PEOPLE AND PLACES*
[Matthew 10:5-6]

PRACTICE 2: PEOPLE AND PLACES

Hopefully by now you're beginning to get a sense of the people or places Jesus is calling you to. If so, it's now time to move onto the second practice of the Pioneer Process. This practice will enable us to understand and begin to make connections with the people and places we feel called to.

Pray

As always, begin this session by humbly coming before God, submitting our own desires and agendas, and asking him to direct our pioneer mission adventure.

Then ask God to speak to you through your imagination. Jesus promises us that his Spirit is going throughout the world testifying and leading people to him (Jn. 15:26-27; 16:5-11). So close your eyes and picture the Spirit (perhaps as a wind or a dove) settling on the places or people he has called you to. As you picture this, reflect on the following questions:

- *Where exactly has the Spirit settled?*

  ....

  ....

  ....

- *Why do you think the Spirit has settled there specifically?*

  ....

  ....

  ....

- *What is the Spirit trying to communicate to you?*

....

....

....

As you dwell on this picture, ask the Spirit to allow you to feel what he feels about this particular people or place.

Report back
Spend some time reporting back on how your prayer practices have been going.

- *What have you found most helpful?*

....

....

....

- *What have you found most challenging?*

....

....

....

- *What has been your experience of prayer-walking?*

....

....

....

- *Are you as individuals and as a group starting to form a regular rhythm of prayer?*

....

....

....

Engage

Ask someone in the group to read Matthew 10:5-6 out loud.

Although this is a very short passage, we'd still encourage you to meditate on it. We often find that it's through the most easily overlooked verses that God speaks to us. So spend 5-10 minutes quietly and slowly reading and re-reading the passage, remaining open to any ideas or questions the Spirit might bring to your mind.

- *What is Jesus saying to you about the mission he's called you to?*

....

....

....

After this period of individual meditation, spend some time as a group sharing what Jesus revealed to you. If you feel the discussion needs a little guidance and direction ask some of the following questions:

- *Why do you think Jesus's instruction to his mission team was so specific?*

  ....
  ....
  ....

- *Do you sense a call yet to a specific place or people?*

  ....
  ....
  ....

- *What would be the danger of expanding this vision too early?*

  ....
  ....
  ....

- *Jesus later expanded this vision to include the people and places he had previously excluded (Acts 1:8). How can we remain open to an expansion of our vision?*

  ....
  ....
  ....

- *Do you think it's significant that Jesus told his followers to go first to their own people, rather than start by crossing cultural and religious barriers?*

....

....

....

- *What might Jesus have been trying to do with his team by giving them local experience first?*

....

....

....

- *Have you had any cross-cultural mission experience?*

....

....

....

- *What were the challenges and rewards?*

....

....

....

- *How does your group's vision relate to the vision Jesus gave his first team?*

....

....

....

Practice

At this point you should have some sense of calling to a particular people or place. Now it's time to start formulating a basic strategy to begin to make connections. While of course we'd encourage you to continue the prayer practices and remain open to the Spirit's guidance at every step, we also believe God speaks to us as we engage in research. Moses, for example, carefully researched the place God had called him to (Num. 13:1-20). Similarly, Paul researched the beliefs of the Athenians before he engaged in mission (Acts 17:16-34).

Intuitive research

If Jesus is calling you to a people or place local to you, you may well already have quite a bit of local knowledge. If so, get a flipchart or large sheet of paper and begin to write down key pieces of information and how you instinctively 'feel' about the place (i.e. your gut reaction). You might also like to think through some of the following questions:

- *What's the population of the place you've been sent to?*

....

....

....

- *What people groups live in the area?*

  ....

  ....

  ....

- *Is there a local 'way of life'?*

  ....

  ....

  ....

- *Where do people naturally gather?*

  ....

  ....

  ....

- *What are the major needs in this area?*

  ....

  ....

  ....

- *What are the main opportunities to serve?*

  ....

  ....

  ....

- *Which local people would have the best understanding of the people or place?*

....
....
....

- *What do you sense God already doing within the people or place?*

....
....
....

Initial research

Once you've considered these questions, begin to engage in some initial research. Break into smaller groups. Give one group some local newspapers, another group the recording of the local news and another group a laptop (you might want to check out www.upmystreet.com and www.statistics.gov.uk). Spend 15 minutes or so researching and then feedback to the group, adding the findings to the sheet of paper.

Now spend some time in prayer asking God to reveal a strategy for reaching the people he's calling you to. You could use some of the prayer practices we explored in the first session. Be sensitive to any spontaneous ideas, thoughts or questions that come to mind.

Deeper research

Sharing local knowledge and engaging in initial research is a quick way of getting a flavour of the people or places we're called to. To really get to grips with the issues, we need to spend time out in the community.

Continue your gathering in a public place in the area or among the people you feel called to (for example in a pub, café, bar, community centre, etc.). Try and go somewhere you perhaps wouldn't normally feel comfortable.

Once you've got a drink and found somewhere to sit (actually, we find standing at the bar a great way of making new connections), pray that God will give you a 'sense' of the place. Then reflect on some of the following questions:

- *Who is in this place?*

....

....

....

- *Is it the sort of place where connections could be made?*

....

....

....

- *Are people gathered in insular groups, or are they mixing freely?*

....

....

....

- *Are there natural gathering points, such as a pool table?*

....
....
....

- *How could you begin to make connections?*

....
....
....

- *What could God already be doing here?*

....
....
....

- *Could you envision a simple church forming in this place?*

....
....
....

Close the evening in prayer. Ask God to speak to you as you continue your various prayer practices, revealing his strategy for reaching the people and place he has called you to.

We've often found that when we've met in public places to discuss our pioneer strategy, God has opened doors for us to share the message and demonstrate the power of his Kingdom. Remember, this travel guide is intended to be as experiential as possible, so take every opportunity to get out into the community and follow God's lead. We've also learnt some vital bits of information simply by sitting in a café or pub and [unintentionally] overhearing a conversation. So arrange for your next meeting to be in a public place.

Truth+Dare

Between now and the next time you gather, we dare you to commit to the truths we've learnt in this session.

- *How will you continue your research?*

....
....
....

We suggest you find a time before your next scheduled gathering when you go out into the community in twos. Spend time in public places simply observing the patterns of life. Speak to shop keepers, the police, MPs, spiritual practitioners or anyone else with good local knowledge. Ask them what they think the needs of the people or places are and how a group like yours can make connections and help out.

- *How will you make connections with people?*

....
....
....

This may involve regularly spending time in a local community centre or bar, joining a local pool league, throwing a house party for your street, or whatever it takes to make connections with the people God has called you to. Be adventurous and think creatively.

- *How will you continue to develop your prayer practices?*

....

....

....

It's important we don't limit ourselves by our own strategies and understandings. We've often found God redirect us and reshape our mission as we've prayed and gone out into the area. So we'd encourage you to keep prayer-walking, announcing the arrival of God's Kingdom, binding the strongman and asking the Spirit to prepare the hearts of the people to receive God's word.

This may all seem like a lot of work, but there's no time limit. You could do this over days, weeks or months, depending on how much time you have to invest in this journey. Some members of your group may be able to commit more time than others. Remember, this is your unique journey.

When you feel you've gained a good understanding of the people or place you're called to and you've started to make some connections, move onto the third practice: 'preach'.

Our Travels

People and place (Pete)

Like Paul the apostle, I believe it's important to 'become all things to all men in order to win some' (1 Cor. 9:22). For me, this has meant spending time with many different people groups.

When God called me to work with young people in the inner-city, I would spend hours with them in the schools, on the streets, in the youth centres and through a project we set up called 'Dream'.

I also felt it was important to actually live in the same community as these young people. This often meant that just going for a pint of milk at the local shop could take up to 3 hours as the young people would question me about why I lived the way I did and about my faith in Jesus. These times were vital in helping me understand their values as I saw first-hand how they spent their time, energy and money.

Over time I became accepted as one of the locals and was increasingly invited into their lives and the lives of their families. This gave me tremendous opportunities to speak about and demonstrate the message of God's Kingdom.

People and place (Tim)

A couple of years ago, my wife, Hannah, and I felt God challenge us to love our neighbours. By this we felt God was calling us not to love our 'neighbours' in a general sense (although of course he meant that as well) but to love our actual neighbours — the people who lived in our street.

Being naturally quite introverted, we didn't instinctively know how to go about this. As we prayed with another Christian couple who lived a few doors down, we felt God prompt us to throw parties for our street. So we began knocking on doors and inviting everyone to a street barbeque. Much to our surprise, the majority of people we spoke to seemed very keen and on the day over 30 people showed up. This led to a number of house parties, Christmas parties, a craft fair, a film club and some great friendships.

Through these connections, we've been able to talk about and demonstrate God's Kingdom on many occasions and have seen God move significantly in our neighbours' lives.

Notes, doodles, sketches…

PRACTICE 3: *PREACH*
[Matthew 10:7]

PRACTICE 3: PREACH

With God's call comes responsibility. Israel had a responsibility to take the Land that God gave them (Josh. 18:3). Similarly, Peter and Paul had a responsibility to preach to the Jews and Gentiles (Gal. 2:7). We, too, have a responsibility to preach the message of God's Kingdom to the people God has called us to.

'Preaching' might sound like a very churchy and culturally insensitive activity to many of you. But all we mean by this word is the activity of sharing with people the good news of God's Kingdom. This third practice will help us begin to think and pray through how we might go about this.

Pray
As always, begin the gathering with prayer. Ask God to speak clearly to you as you consider how to communicate his message to the people or places he's called you to.

When the Early Church sensed God giving a person a specific call, they commissioned them for that work. They did this by fasting and laying hands on them (Acts 13:1-3). Observe a fast together. Then when you end your fast with a meal, commission each other by laying hands on each other.

Report back
Spend some time reporting back on your journey so far.

- *How are your prayer practices going?*

....

....

....

- *How are you getting on with your research into the people and places you've been sent to?*

  ....
  ....
  ....

- *What discoveries have you made and how might they shape your mission strategy?*

  ....
  ....
  ....

- *What connections are you starting to make in the local community?*

  ....
  ....
  ....

Engage
Ask someone in the group to read Matthew 10:7 out loud.

As with our previous passage, this one's short, but we'd encourage you to meditate on it. Spend time quietly and slowly reading and re-reading the passage, remaining open to any ideas or questions the Spirit might bring to your mind.

- *What is Jesus saying to you about communicating his message to the people and places he's called you to?*

....

....

....

Spend time as a group sharing what Jesus revealed to you. Use some of the following questions if you need to.

- *In what different ways can we 'preach' the message of God's coming Kingdom?*

....

....

....

- *What have been your experiences of communicating the message of God's Kingdom?*

....

....

....

- *Have you experienced occasions where your message has been misunderstood?*

....

....

....

- *What did you learn from that experience?*

....

....

....

- *How might our method of communication change depending on where we are and who we're with?*

....

....

....

- *Do you already have a sense of how (or how not) to communicate the message to the people or place you feel called to?*

....

....

....

- *Can you think of 101 ways of reaching out to the people or places God is calling you to?*

....

....

....

- *Jesus told us to preach 'the Kingdom of heaven is near'. What do you understand by this?*

....

....

....

- *How could we translate this message into language understandable to the people we're called to?*

....

....

....

Case study

We can see from the book of Acts how the Early Church went about translating their message to make it relevant to their audience.

God gave Peter a call to the Jews. We can see him preaching the message of the Kingdom to them during the Jewish festival of Pentecost. Read Acts 2:14-41 to see how he did this.

Paul, on the other hand, was called to preach to the Gentiles (Gal. 2:7). We can see how he did this in Athens, when he engaged with Greek philosophers. Read Acts 17:16-34 to see how he went about this.

- *How did Peter's message differ from Paul's in terms of their starting points and religious and cultural references?*

....
....
....

- *What elements of their message were the same?*

....
....
....

- *What lessons can we learn about how we should 'preach' to the people and places we're called to?*

....
....
....

Practice
Now that you have a sense of calling to a particular people or place and you're starting to make connections, it's time to begin to communicate the message of God's Kingdom.

Sharing spiritual conversations
To begin with, find ways of bringing up conversation with the people in the places where you've been hanging out. You can begin with easy conversation starters like discussing the weather or what's happening in the news.

It's important to establish a common rapport. So if the people you are engaging with have children, it's good to ask their names and ages. If they go to college, you could ask about the courses they're studying and so on.

Be a good listener. A quick glance at the gospels reveals just how good Jesus was at listening and asking questions (Luke 2:46).

Below are a few suggestions of the kind of questions you could use to stimulate spiritual conversation:

- *On a scale of 1-10, how fulfilled are you in life?*
- *What do you think about Jesus?*
- *What do you think happens when you die?*
- *If you could ask God one question, what would it be?*
- *If you could know God personally, would you be interested?*

- *What other spiritual conversation starters can you think of?*

....

....

....

Sharing your story
The idea of sharing our faith can be scary for some people, but it really shouldn't be. Sharing our faith is simply telling our story. This story only really has three elements.

1. Your life before coming to faith
2. How you came to faith
3. Your life after coming to faith

Jesus was convinced that this simple practice of sharing our story would be powerfully used to further his Kingdom. In Revelation, a heavenly voice announces that the devil will be overcome by Jesus's victory on the cross *and* by the word of our testimony (Rev. 12:11).

Of course, we should never impose our story on people. Instead, we should earn our right to talk by showing a genuine interest in the stories of others. Peter, for example, was careful to give Cornelius an opportunity to share his story before he shared his own (Acts 10:25-34).

Get into groups of two or three and share your faith stories. Make sure you don't spend more than three minutes each and don't use any religious language.

Sharing Jesus's story
Sharing your story naturally puts the emphasis on you. But let's think about the story from Jesus's perspective.

Staying in your twos and threes, try and answer the following questions:

• *Who is Jesus?*

....

....

....

• *Why did he die?*

....

....

....

- *What makes you think he came back to life?*

....

....

....

Your answers don't have to be 'academic'. Your experiences are just as valid.

Feed your thoughts back to the whole group and try to come to a consensus on who Jesus is, why he died and why we believe he was resurrected.

Sharing in the Spirit's story

Jesus said he would send his Spirit to go throughout the world convicting people of sin, righteousness and judgement (Jn. 16:8-11). So, one of the Spirit's primary roles is to lead people to faith in Jesus.

- *Were you aware of the Spirit's activity in your life before you came to faith (either at the time or in hindsight)?*

....

....

....

Jesus said he would send his Spirit to testify about him. Immediately after this, he said we too must testify about him (Jn. 15:26-27). The Spirit is always one step ahead of us. Our job is simply to follow the Spirit's lead and share our story and the story of Jesus with the people the Spirit leads us to.

- *Have you ever had the experience of sharing your faith with someone who already seemed to be responding to God?*

....

....

....

The book of Acts is full of stories of 'divine appointments' where Jesus's Spirit guided one of the apostles to a person who was open to their message. Think, for example, of the stories of Philip and the Ethiopian, Peter and Cornelius, or Paul and Lydia. On these occasions, the apostles didn't create opportunities, they were simply sensitive to where the Spirit was leading and what he was prompting them to say.

- *How do you think we can identify people who are already open to the Spirit?*

....

....

....

Being guided by the Spirit to people who are open to the message of the Kingdom doesn't mean we can sit back passively. We still need to get out there, be around and connect with new people. And it doesn't mean that 'divine appointments' will be our entire pioneer experience. The apostles also had their fair share of encounters with people who definitely weren't interested in their message!

Helping people share in Jesus's story

We've found that with a little experience you'll soon find yourself naturally sharing your story with people. The next level of challenge, however, is intentionally guiding someone to faith. If we sense someone is showing interest, we need to be prepared to challenge them to follow this interest up.

Get back into your groups of twos or threes and discuss how you were led to faith.

- *How could we help someone who's showing interest to take the next step to faith in Jesus?*

....

....

....

We've tried many different approaches to helping people along in their faith journey. These have nearly always involved drawing together small groups of seekers. We've then used pre-packaged seeker courses such as *Alpha*, *Christianity Explored* or *Glad You Asked*. More recently, however, we've begun to put together our own courses so we can better tailor them to the people interested. This has included simple Bible studies based on the stories of Jesus, through to meditation courses for spiritual seekers.

- *If you felt the time was right to help someone start praying to Jesus, how might you guide their first prayer?*

....

....

....

Remember that faith is a journey, so encourage a simple prayer that reflects where the person is. Ultimately, we would want to see all the elements of Christian initiation (faith, repentance, baptism in water and the Spirit). But we need to be sensitive to what the Spirit is doing in a person at this particular time. We've had a great deal of success, for example, in guiding people in a simple prayer that says that while they're not entirely sure of who Jesus is, they're open to him revealing himself to them. We've found that Jesus is all too happy to answer this sort of honest prayer!

Truth+Dare

For many of you, putting these truths into practice will really feel like a dare! But be encouraged, Jesus promises us he's with us when we go out with the intention of making disciples (Mt. 28:19-20). So pray for boldness and step out in faith!

- *How will you go about spending regular time among the people or in the places God has called you to?*

....

....

....

- *How will you stay open to the possibility of 'divine appointments' among the people God has called you to?*

....

....

....

- *How will you remind yourself to regularly pray for the people you're starting to make connections with?*

   ....
   ....
   ....

- *How will you go about working through your 101 ways of reaching out to the people and places God has called you to?*

   ....
   ....
   ....

- *How will you remind yourself to regularly pray for boldness?*

   ....
   ....
   ....

When you feel your connections with people are deepening and you're starting to get opportunities to share your story and the story of Jesus, move onto the next practice.

Our Travels

Preach (Pete)
I quickly learnt that before preaching the message of God's Kingdom, it was essential to understand the culture of the people group I was called to. So I'd begin to think about what connecting points there were between the gospel and these people.

When we began spreading the gospel with young people in urban gangs, for example, we used rap, hip-hop and drum'n'bass music and later grime and dubstep. We would drive onto an estate and my friend would Emcee about Jesus out of the window of the car. We would then begin to share our stories of what Jesus had done for us. This seemed to go down really well with the youth and there was no lack of questions!

Preach (Pete and Tim)
As we prayed together, we both felt God prompt us to go to a local Buddhist Meditation Centre. The centre had recently opened a café so we went in and quietly prayed.

Neither of us had much previous experience of Buddhism and so we didn't instinctively know how to connect with this community. Over the weeks, however, God kept giving us opportunities to speak with Buddhist monks, nuns and spiritual seekers, and listen to their stories (many of whom it turned out had come from a Christian background!). As we listened, we began to notice reoccurring themes, such as a desire for community, purity, peace and a holistic spirituality. This allowed us to share stories of our experiences of Jesus and of a simple, relational form of church.

Notes, doodles, sketches…

PRACTICE 4: *POWER*
[Matthew 10:8]

PRACTICE 4: POWER

This practice refers to a key component of the way Jesus and the Early Church went about pioneer mission. The power in question is the power given to us by the Spirit of Jesus to demonstrate the reality of God's Kingdom.

Pray
Begin your gathering by spending a few minutes quietly sitting in God's presence. Ask God to bring to mind anything that we might need forgiveness for. Encourage the group to turn the palms of their hands down as they release their sin to God. Then encourage them to turn their palms up and pray to be refilled with the Spirit and with power.

Report back
Spend some time reporting back to the group on how your pioneer mission has been going.

- *Has the group developed a regular rhythm of prayer yet?*

....

....

....

- *How have you been getting on with communicating the news of God's Kingdom within the places and to the people God has called you to?*

....

....

....

- *Which aspects have been going well and which have you found challenging?*

....
....
....

Engage

Ask someone in the group to read Matthew 10:8 out loud.

Spend time meditating on this verse. Allow the Spirit to bring questions and ideas to your mind.

- *What's Jesus saying to you about how he would have you demonstrate the power of God's Kingdom?*

....
....
....

Spend time as a group sharing what Jesus has revealed to you. Ask some of the following questions if you feel the discussion needs some direction:

- *Have you ever experienced a demonstration of the Spirit's power?*

....
....
....

- *Do you believe God still wants to use us in this way?*

....

....

....

- *Can you personally imagine being used in this way?*

....

....

....

- *Why do you think demonstrations of power seem less common in the Western church today than in other parts of the world?*

....

....

....

- *What concerns would you have in praying for healing or deliverance?*

....

....

....

- *What sort of impact do you think a demonstration of such power would have on the people and places you're called to?*

....

....

....

- *Why do you think Jesus specifically mentions leprosy?*

....

....

....

- *What might a modern equivalent of healing someone from leprosy be?*

....

....

....

Practice

At this stage, you should have started communicating the message of God's Kingdom to the people you feel called to. Effective communication of the Kingdom requires more than just words, however. It requires a demonstration of power.

Power for all believers

There are specific gifts of miracles, healing and discerning of spirits (1 Cor. 12:9-11), just as there's a specific apostolic gift.

But like the apostolic gift, we're all called to step out in faith in these gifts as the Spirit leads us.

Jesus promised that if we have faith, we'll do even greater things than he did (Jn. 14:12)! The Early Church took Jesus's words very seriously, and healings and deliverance became an important part of the way they went about pioneer mission. Paul, for example, wrote to the Corinthian church and reminded them that his 'message and...preaching were not with wise and persuasive words, but with a demonstration of the Spirit's power' (1 Cor. 2:4).

- *Is anyone in the group aware they have a specific gift of miracles, healing or discerning of spirits?*

....

....

....

Get into groups of two or three and lay hands on each other. Ask God to bless each one of you with a gift to equip you for mission. Then spend time quietly listening to God to discern what these gifts might be.

Power for effective witness
Miracles are an important part of mission because they're evangelistic (i.e. they point to God). Miracles are also prophetic as they give a glimpse of God's future Kingdom breaking into the present. Jesus believed that healings and deliverance were a sign that Satan's reign was coming to an end and that God's Kingdom was advancing (Lk. 10:18-20). This is as true and as needed today as it was in the time of the Early Church.

- *Think of a miracle you've experienced or heard about. How did it point to Jesus, the coming of God's Kingdom and the end of Satan's reign?*

....

....

....

- *If miracles point to the coming of God's Kingdom, why don't they seem as common today as they did for the Early Church?*

....

....

....

Of course, there are many reasons why miracles might not seem as common today. These can range from the scepticism that comes from living in a 'rational' culture, to churches not effectively equipping Christians and limiting their expectation of miracles to the confines of Christian meetings. Whatever the reason, we're convinced biblically and through our own experience that God still wants to demonstrate the reality of his Kingdom through miracles. There are, however, four problems that we, and others we know, have had to overcome.

Lack of knowledge

When we start moving into healing and deliverance, we need to be very closely attuned to the Spirit's guidance, as there are no formulas. So it's vital we're regularly engaged in the various prayer practices. There are, however, a number of principles revealed in the New Testament.

- *Can you think of the different ways in which people were healed in the New Testament?*

....

....

....

- *What can we learn from this?*

....

....

....

Jesus and the first disciples healed through forgiveness of sins, deliverance from demons, lying on top of someone, having no physical contact with the person at all, rebuking disease and using mud, spit, oil, handkerchiefs, aprons and even shadows!

This great variety in healing shows us two things. First, we need to discern and confront the cause of an illness, which can be sin, demonic oppression or simply the result of living in a fallen world. Second, we need to be sensitive to how the Spirit is telling us to go about administering healing.

- *Have you ever had an encounter with someone you suspected was being influenced by demonic spirits?*

....

....

....

In our experience, demonic encounters can come about in two main ways. First, we've experienced demonic opposition in someone whose path we've crossed while on mission. This has manifested in unprovoked aggression, verbal abuse, simply blocking our path, or on rare occasions satanic language. This is all simply a crude strategy to stop your pioneering work, and we'd advise you to politely walk on. If you do feel threatened, then you can 'bind' the demonic spirit in the person, just as Jesus bound the 'strongman' (Mt. 12:29). You may sense, however, that the Holy Spirit is urging you to set the person free, as Jesus did when confronted by the man possessed by Legion (Lk. 8:26-35).

Second, we've found that as we've made connections with people, we've observed 'strongholds' in their lives. These can be persistent sinful thought patterns or behaviours, addictions or other forms of destructive behaviour. Where the Spirit has revealed an underlying demonic cause, we've sought to deliver that person.

- *How did Jesus and the Early Church go about freeing people from demonic oppression?*

....

....

....

It's our understanding that demons can't just randomly afflict us. They need a right to be there. So Paul told the Ephesian Christians, for example, 'not to let the sun go down while you're still angry, and do not give the devil a foothold' (Eph. 4:26-27). The Greek word for 'foothold' is *topos* and literally means a physical place, a base from which to make further advances. So a persistent sinful attitude or behaviour can give a demon a foothold. A demon's 'name' will often reflect its right to be there or the symptom it's causing in its victim. The key to breaking this hold is to discern the right that the demon has to afflict a person. You can then lead them in confession of that sin and in expressing their desire to be free. You can then command the demon to leave in Jesus's name.

As with healing, however, there were occasions when Jesus and the Early Church simply told a demon to leave without any investigation into the reason for its presence. So, as with all aspects of pioneer mission, you must remain open and sensitive to the Holy Spirit.

Lack of experience
Any new experience can lead to nervousness — and for many people an overtly supernatural encounter would be a very new experience. Added to this is the context of pioneer mission among people you're probably not entirely comfortable with. This could understandably lead to some hesitancy!

Our advice would be to ease into it. Why not begin by praying for each other before you begin to pray for people in the context of mission?

Spend some time exploring whether anyone in the group needs physical healing or is feeling oppressed in any way. If everyone feels ready, why not lay hands on each other and perhaps anoint with oil and pray for healing or deliverance. If no one in the group feels they need prayer, why not discuss whether the group knows anyone they would feel comfortable praying for.

Lack of opportunity

When you're first making connections with people, you may not be aware of any obvious need for healing or deliverance.

- *Have you been aware of the need for deliverance in the people you've been connecting with?*

....
....
....

- *If not, why do you think the need for deliverance doesn't seem as obvious in our culture as it did in Jesus's time?*

....
....
....

It's important to remember that, like any good military strategist, the devil will try and do as much damage as possible before anyone realises he's there. Our 'rational' western culture has allowed the devil to do much of his work unnoticed. Jesus lived in a very spiritually attuned culture. This coupled with the fact that demons knew they couldn't hide from him meant that Jesus encountered much more spiritual warfare than we often do.

- *What practically can we do to become more aware of the need for healing and deliverance in the people we're connecting with?*

....

....

....

We've found that it's important to begin by simply listening to people's stories. Then, as we become aware of their everyday struggles, we can begin to offer prayer. This may be as simple as offering to pray for God's peace for someone who's feeling anxious. We've found that a simple prayer like this can lead to a profound experience of God and may bring deeper needs to the surface.

As we get to know people more intimately, we'll almost certainly become aware of deeper issues. At this point they'll already be open to the offer of prayer and we can begin to engage in more overt spiritual warfare as the Spirit leads us.

Fear of failure
Another common cause for hesitancy is the fear that when you've plucked up the courage to pray for someone, nothing will happen! And it's true that even in the faith-charged atmosphere of the Early Church not everyone was healed. Timothy, for example, continued to struggle with a dodgy stomach (1 Tim. 5:23) — even though he was best mates with one of church history's great healers, Paul the apostle!

- *Have you ever prayed for someone's healing or deliverance and seemingly nothing happened?*

....

....

....

- *How did you come to terms with this?*

....

....

....

A lack of knowledge and experience can be part of the problem. On one occasion, the disciples failed to deliver someone from a spirit because they hadn't discerned that on that particular occasion they needed to pray and fast (Mk. 9:29). Even Jesus had to persist in prayer on one occasion before someone was completely healed (Mk. 8:22-26).

There are, of course, occasions when we do 'everything right' and the person is still not healed. All we can do is trust that God knows what he's doing. If we felt prompted by the Spirit to pray for a person, then we can be assured the Spirit is doing something even if we can't see it. But if we want to see God's Kingdom demonstrated in power we must step out in faith and persist in the practice of praying for healing and deliverance. You may not *see* something happen every time, but there will be occasions when you do. And trust us — it's worth waiting for!

Truth+Dare

We think the truth of the importance of healing and deliverance is pretty clear (if you still need convincing just read through the gospels and Acts). So we dare you to do it!

- *How will you continue your commitment to spending time among the people or in the place God has called you to?*

....

....

....

- *How will you stay open to 'divine appointments'?*

....

....

....

- *How will you go about offering simple prayers for people?*

....

....

....

- *How will you stay open to the possibility of praying for healing and deliverance?*

....

....

....

When you're ready move onto the next practice: 'Person of Peace'.

Our Travels

Power (Pete)

Sometimes when we'd talk about Jesus to gangs of young people in the inner-city, they'd just laugh and say "you can't prove there's a God!" After this had gone on for a while, I sensed God urging me to set a challenge. So I started saying to them "I can prove God exists" — to which they would naturally reply "How? Go on then!" So I would lay hands on them (with their permission!) and pray that Jesus would reveal himself to them. I did this many times and every time something happened and the young people had an encounter with Jesus.

Power (Pete and Tim)

On one of our first visits to the Buddhist Meditation Centre, we got into a conversation with a Buddhist monk. Like many of the people we'd met there, he'd come from a Christian background, but had rejected it on the basis that it wasn't 'spiritual'.

As the conversation progressed and he spoke more about the 'genuine spiritually' he'd discovered in Buddhism, we noticed he was in physical pain. It turned out he had an ongoing back problem that the doctors could no longer treat. We asked if he'd like us to pray for his healing in Jesus's name, and he hesitantly agreed. Although nothing seemed to happen right there and then, we visited the next day and he said he'd had a rare pain-free day. This led to a two-hour conversation about Jesus spirituality — the real thing!

Notes, doodles, sketches…

PRACTICE 5: *PERSON OF PEACE*
[Matthew 10:9-11; 40-42]

PRACTICE 5: PERSON OF PEACE

So far we've been exploring how to find anyone receptive to our message. In terms of establishing a new Jesus-centred community, however, there's a specific type of person we're hoping to find. Luke calls this person a 'man of peace' (Lk. 10:6), although we prefer to use the more inclusive 'Person of Peace'.

Pray
After you've committed this session to God, spend some time praying again to be refilled with God's Spirit. Pray in particular that God will give you an increase in your ability to discern the specific individuals the Spirit is leading you to.

The Hebrew and Greek words for 'Spirit' are the same as 'wind' and 'breathe'. Try slowing down and deepening your breathing. Then imagine breathing out your fears and own agendas, and breathing in God's Spirit.

Report back
Spend some time reporting back to the group about how your pioneer mission adventure has been developing.

- *How have you been getting on 'preaching' the message to the people or places God has called you to?*

....

....

....

- *Have you seen anyone begin to show signs of responding?*

  ....

  ....

  ....

- *Have you been able to offer prayer to anyone?*

  ....

  ....

  ....

- *Have you had any opportunities to demonstrate the power of the Kingdom through healing and deliverance?*

  ....

  ....

  ....

Engage

Ask someone in the group to read Matthew 10:9-11 and 40-42 out loud. Spend time meditating on these verses. Allow the Spirit to bring questions and ideas to your mind.

- *What is Jesus saying to you about People of Peace?*

  ....

  ....

  ....

Spend time sharing together as a group. You can use some of the following questions if you feel they would be helpful.

- *Why do you think Jesus told his team not to take any money or provisions with them on their pioneering journey?*

  ....
  ....
  ....

- *How could this relate to finding a person who will welcome you into their home?*

  ....
  ....
  ....

- *Are you better at giving or receiving hospitality?*

  ....
  ....
  ....

- *Why do you think Jesus linked the offer of hospitality with a person open to the message of the Kingdom?*

  ....
  ....
  ....

- *How does finding a Person of Peace relate more to pioneer mission and starting a new Jesus-centred community, than to friendship evangelism and adding people to an existing community?*

  ....

  ....

  ....

- *How do you feel about Jesus's command to leave those who don't welcome us or listen to our message?*

  ....

  ....

  ....

- *What distinction does this command reveal between 'friendship evangelism' and pioneer mission?*

  ....

  ....

  ....

Case studies

In order to more clearly define a Person of Peace, we're going to look at the People of Peace Jesus and the Early Church found.

Get into groups of two or three and take one or two of the following passages each to discuss.

- Matthew (Mt. 9:9-13)
- The Samaritan woman (Jn. 4:7-42)
- Cornelius (Acts 10:1-48)
- Lydia (Acts 16:13-15, 40)
- Priscilla and Aquila (Acts 18:1-3; 18-28)

Feed back to the group what you've learnt from these passages about what makes a Person of Peace.

These case studies show that a Person of Peace is someone who offers you hospitality and is open to the message you bring. But more than that, they're a key person in the place or among the people you've been sent to. Their significance lies in the fact they're an influential person at the centre of their household or social circle. And, importantly, they're someone who will use their influence to bring their friends, family and social circle together to hear your message. So rather than having to reach a number of individuals to form a new community, we reach a Person of Peace and they then reach many others.

Practice
At this stage of the journey, you should have formed good connections with the people you feel called to. You should also be communicating the message of the Kingdom and demonstrating it with simple prayers and in power. If so, then you're in a good position to find a Person of Peace.

How to find People of Peace
As we've seen from the passages we just looked at, finding a Person of Peace is an important step in pioneer mission and forming new Jesus-centred communities. So it's essential we start to consider how we go about locating such a person.

- *From the Matthew 10 passage and the case studies, how did Jesus and the Early Church go about finding People of Peace?*

....

....

....

Jesus and the Early Church found People of Peace by praying, spending time with people, preaching and demonstrating the power of the Kingdom. If someone they connected with responded to their message with hospitality and by gathering their friends, family or social network, they were a Person of Peace.

There were occasions, however, when the Spirit specifically guided someone to a Person of Peace. We see this with Peter and Cornelius, for example. This is yet another reminder that we need to be sensitive to the guidance of the Spirit.

Spend some time feeding back to the group about how you've been getting on preaching and demonstrating the power of God's Kingdom.

- *Have you come across anyone you feel might be a Person of Peace?*

....

....

....

What to do when you find People of Peace

Once we've found someone we think might be a Person of Peace, we need to think through how to make the most of this opportunity.

- *From the Matthew 10 reading and the case studies, what should we do when we find a Person of Peace?*

....

....

....

The most important thing to do when you've found a Person of Peace is to regularly invest time in them. Remember, these people are key influencers through whom the message of the Kingdom can spread to an entire family or social network.

Once you've made a good connection with such a person, the process of making disciples begins. We believe discipleship starts before someone actually comes to faith. Jesus, for example, discipled his followers long before they realised exactly who he was.

- *From the case studies, what initial steps did Jesus and the Early Church take to make disciples?*

....

....

....

Jesus and the Early Church spent time with the Person of Peace. They listened to their story, shared their own story and the story of Jesus — and demonstrated it in power. This led to faith and repentance, expressed through baptism in water and the Spirit. Basically, they helped to transition the person from an initial interest in Jesus through to a fully initiated disciple.

- *In what practical ways could you begin to reach the Person of Peace's social and family networks?*

....

....

....

It's important you explain to the Person of Peace from the start that as Jesus's followers we're called to make disciples. Consequently, they should immediately begin to consider how to share their experience of Jesus with others.

There are a few simple things you can do to begin to help the Person of Peace reach their social networks. Most simply, we begin by asking them if there's anyone else they'd like to bring along the next time we meet. We'll then organise a simple Bring+Share where we share meals and stories.

After this, we've found that a baptism party is an excellent way to introduce their social network to the message of the Kingdom. In the New Testament, water baptism occurred very soon after someone came to faith (often immediately), as a sign of the washing away of their sin and their death and resurrection in Jesus. So why wait? When the Person of Peace comes to faith, organise a baptism party (we've used everything from a bath to the sea) and encourage them to invite their friends and family. We try to make it a fun celebration with food, drink and music, with the Person of

Peace's story and baptism at the centre. This can have a profound impact on their family and friends.

We'd then encourage People of Peace to form their own groups, where they can meet with members of their family and social network to talk about spirituality and share stories.

- *What should we do with people who are open to our message, but who aren't specifically People of Peace?*

....

....

....

We should treat everyone as a potential Person of Peace. Peter said, for example, when he preached to the crowd at Pentecost about the gift of the Holy Spirit 'This promise is not just for you, but for your whole household!' (Acts 2:38-39). So every new believer should be encouraged to reach their circle of influence. Some people, however, are better connected and more influential and so are better able to reach their social networks. These are the People of Peace Jesus spoke about.

This isn't to say we're not interested in people who aren't People of Peace. Of course, we still hope and pray they come to faith. But rather than forming a new Jesus community around them, we introduce them to an existing community to be discipled. We must be wise in how we use our time. Indeed, Jesus told his pioneering team to not even 'greet anyone on the road' (Lk. 10:4). So rather than discipling many individuals, our aim is to disciple a few People of Peace who can then disciple many others (2 Tim 2:2). Jesus led a man to faith, for example, who spread the message to his family and then to ten cities! (Mk. 5:19-20).

Truth+Dare

How are you going to respond to these truths?

• *How are you going to commit to searching and praying for People of Peace?*

....
....
....

• *When you find them, how will you go about spending regular time discipling them and helping them reach their family and social networks?*

....
....
....

When you've found and begun to disciple a Person of Peace, and they start to share their story with their social networks, move onto the next practice.

Our Travels

Person of Peace (Pete)

In the early days, I didn't quite understand the Person of Peace concept. As I hung out, prayed and preached, I knew I was looking for 'key people' but I didn't quite know what I'd do when I found them.

On the first estate I worked on, God highlighted a central family. Over time, I was able to get to know all the members and they welcomed me into their home and into their lives. I didn't realise it at the time, but I'd found both a person and a home of peace.

Looking back, I wish I'd known then what I know now. I'd have intentionally discipled the Person of Peace in a weekly coaching relationship and encouraged her to gather her family together to form a simple church. Then I'd have withdrawn so that the Person of Peace could continue to lead her family.

We now regularly follow this practice and have seen its transforming power.

Person of Peace (Tim)

As soon as I became a Christian, groups seemed to form around me. Whether it was at university, work or in the areas where I lived, I seemed to naturally draw people together to explore Christian spirituality, pray, be accountable to each other, or study the Bible. It's only since I've discovered the concept of the Person of Peace that I've realised that was who I was!

Notes, doodles, sketches…

PRACTICE 6: *PLANT*
[Matthew 10:11-15]

PRACTICE 6: PLANT

Once we've found a Person of Peace and they're beginning to lead members of their family and social network to faith, we need to begin to form a new spiritual community. This community must be shaped in such a way that it becomes a spiritual family that will itself go on to form new Jesus-centred communities.

Although the New Testament doesn't specifically use the phrase 'church planting', Paul talks about planting 'seed' (1 Cor. 3:6), which we know is the Word of God (Mt. 13:3-23). So when we use the word 'Plant' we're referring to planting ourselves with the Person of Peace and planting the word — beginning with the basic teachings and practices among the group they've drawn together. This will allow a Jesus-centred community to form organically.

Pray
The Holy Spirit is mentioned dozens of times in the book of Acts, and most of these occurrences are directly connected to mission. So clearly it's important we maintain our sensitivity to the Spirit's guidance. Paul told the Ephesian churches, however, that we can grieve the Spirit (Eph. 4:30). So we believe it's important to develop a regular practice of confession and refilling.

Spend some time quietly waiting in God's presence. Ask him to reveal to you if you've grieved the Spirit in any way. After a time of confession, pray for a refilling of the Spirit. You may find it helpful to symbolise this in some way by, for example, anointing with oil or lighting a candle.

Report back

Spend some time reporting back on how your pioneer mission is going so far.

- *Have you found a Person of Peace yet?*

....

....

....

- *Have you started meeting regularly to coach them?*

....

....

....

- *Are they beginning to reach out to their family and social network?*

....

....

....

Engage

Ask someone in the group to read Matthew 10:11-15 out loud.

Spend some time meditating on these verses. Allow the Spirit to bring questions and ideas to your mind.

- *What is Jesus saying to you about forming a new Jesus-centred community?*

....

....

....

Spend some time sharing together as a group. You can use some of the following questions if you feel they would be helpful.

- *In what way do you think these verses relate to both the Person of Peace and to the forming of a new church?*

....

....

....

- *If it's the Person of Peace who expresses their interest in your message by offering hospitality and it's around them that a church forms, where is that church likely to meet?*

....

....

....

- *What practical advantages would meeting in homes have given the Early Church?*

  ....

  ....

  ....

- *What would meeting in a home say symbolically about the nature of the Christian community?*

  ....

  ....

  ....

- *What has been your experience of meeting in homes, compared to meeting in dedicated church buildings?*

  ....

  ....

  ....

- *What do you think are the pros and cons of both?*

  ....

  ....

  ....

- *What would you anticipate as being the biggest challenges in forming a new community?*

....

....

....

Practice

At this stage, you should have made a good connection with someone you believe to be a Person of Peace, who in turn is reaching out to their friends and family. If you're at this stage, it's now time to consider how we can move on to form a new Jesus-centred community.

Forming *new* churches

Churches can often become more interested in evangelistic strategies and pioneer mission when numbers in their congregations begin to decline. While falling numbers can act as a useful wakeup call to the church, we believe pioneer mission is not about adding new people to existing churches. Rather, it's about establishing new churches.

- *Why do you think pioneer mission requires the forming of new churches rather than adding people to existing ones?*

....

....

....

The aim of pioneer mission is to take the message of God's Kingdom to unreached people groups and places. So the Person of Peace isn't an individual convert to be added to a church, but an access point through which the message can penetrate a whole new people group. This people group can then shape a new Jesus community that uniquely reflects their faith and culture.

Forming *small* churches

The Early Church was composed of many small house churches. Some scholars have suggested the church organised itself in this way due to persecution and a lack of resources. While it's true that small churches have proved to be more resistant to persecution, we believe the church organised itself in this way for a much more fundamental reason.

- *In terms of community, discipleship and mission, why do you think it would be best to form a number of small house churches, rather than trying to grow a few large churches?*

....

....

....

Paul the apostle believed that the reason believers needed to meet together was to mature as disciples (1 Cor. 14:12; Eph. 4:11-12). In order for this to occur, he expected everyone to discover their gifts and contribute them when the church met together (1 Cor. 14:26). And for this to work, gatherings had to be kept small (a typical first-century house would hold no more than thirty people).

The Early Church also saw itself as a spiritual family (e.g. Gal. 6:10). Consequently, meetings were highly relational, centring on a shared meal. This depth of community meant that meetings had to be kept small.

The Early Church was also committed to mission. For the church to remain effectively engaged in its desire to make disciples of all nations, it had to remain flexible and able to respond quickly to changing internal (Acts 6:1-6) and external circumstances (Acts 15:1-21). Equally, it had to keep its overheads low, so that resources could be channelled into mission (e.g. Phil. 4:16-20). This meant keeping the structures of the church small and simple.

Forming *networked* churches
Although the first Christians met together for informal gatherings in homes, they were considered to be fully-fledged churches in their own right. These house churches didn't exist in isolation, however. Instead they networked together.

- *What do you think would be the advantages of networking house churches together?*

....

....

....

Many people seem concerned that house churches don't have sufficient accountability. Actually, we've found that house churches often have a greater depth of accountability than larger traditionally structured churches. That's because the relationships in house churches tend to be deeper and more intimate. Nevertheless, we do think that networking churches together provides another level of accountability. So, for example, one group may find they have a particularly gifted teacher. That teacher can be 'shared' with other groups, or can organise resources and training to help churches engage with the Bible more deeply.

We also believe it's important that churches network with each other to establish a citywide identity. The New Testament vision of church was of a global Body of Christ, which had local expressions. So, for example, Paul wrote to individual churches that met in a particular home (e.g. Rom. 16:3-5). But he also wrote to the church in a particular city (e.g. 1 Cor. 1:2), which consisted of a number of these smaller house churches. He also wrote to a number of churches in a particular region (e.g. Gal. 1:1).

- *How could we go about networking houses churches together?*

....

....

....

As we've already said, those with particular gifts such as teaching are called not just to teach others, but also to equip Christians to teach each other (Eph. 4:11-12; Col. 3:16). So the Early Church had apostles, prophets, evangelists, pastors and teachers, who would write to and visit the various house churches to equip them (e.g. Acts 14:21-22). The Early Church also occasionally brought all the house churches together for citywide gatherings for specific purposes (e.g. 1 Cor. 14:23).

Forming *self-sustaining* churches

One of the most surprising elements of Paul's strategy for forming new churches was the speed with which he moved on to another area of work (sometimes within just a few months). Yet he seemed confident that these new churches would not only survive but would grow and multiply.

- *How do you think we can begin to move from meeting with a Person of Peace to coaching them to form a self-sustaining church?*

....

....

....

Once you've made a good connection with a Person of Peace, and their friends and family are showing some interest, you can start to encourage them to begin meeting together regularly.

We believe it's essential, however, to make it clear from the start that you won't be the leader of this church. Instead, you'll only attend in the early stages in order to model church life for them. They'll be facilitating this church and will be looking to Jesus to lead it through his word and Spirit. You'll then leave to find other People of Peace.

An easy way to remember the pioneer's role is through the acronym SHOW. First the pioneer will 'Show' the basic teaching and practice through their example. It's important that we do this in a simple way so it's easy for the group to imitate (for example, avoid long elaborate prayers and in-depth Bible teaching). Then the pioneer will 'Help' the group as they begin to practice these basics themselves (for example, begin to ask them to pray or read the Bible). Next we should step back and 'Observe' the person we're coaching as they practice the basics without our assistance. Finally we 'Withdraw' from the group. We've found that it's vital to get the timing of our departure just right, so we need to be sensitive to the Spirit's leading. If we leave too soon, the group may drift from the basics and could soon stall or even die. But on the other hand, if we stay too long, the group can easily become dependent on us and local leaders won't emerge.

This is not to say, of course, that our departure will mean the new church will be left entirely on its own to fend for itself. You can still meet with the Person of Peace (or whoever begins to facilitate the church gatherings) to coach them. And you'll be connecting this church with the wider network of churches as it develops.

Forming *self-reproducing* churches

For our message to spread quickly and widely, the churches we form must be reproducible. The more complex and reliant on professionals the church becomes, the less able it is to multiply. Consequently, we need to form 'Simple Churches'. Paul the apostle, for example, formed churches whose activities were so simple he was able to leave them relatively soon after their formation (e.g. Acts 18:11). These churches were not only able to largely fend for themselves, but also to reproduce themselves.

- *How can we simplify the key activities of the church, such as prayer and engaging with the Bible, so that anyone can do them?*

....

....

....

Church gatherings don't have to be led by gifted musicians and preachers (as great a blessing as they can be). Actually, the Early Church gatherings were very different from this. They were informal, relational and interactive. Jesus set the Early Church a model for gatherings at the Last Supper.

- *What different elements were involved in the meeting described in Mark 14:17-26?*

....

....

....

- *How did the meeting create a relational, informal and interactive atmosphere?*

....

....

....

Jesus modelled a gathering that involved eating, spending time together, teaching, questions, prayer and the use of symbolism and movement. Being based around a meal provided an informal setting, which allowed for a relational and interactive experience. This was the model the Early Church adopted. So Paul was adamant that everyone should be contributing their unique gifts when the church gathered (1 Cor. 14:26). There was no place for passive observers.

We've found that groups are generally quite good at learning to worship together, but it's when they approach the Bible they feel inadequate and ill-equipped. While gifted Bible teachers can be a great blessing to a network of house churches, the New Testament does expect us to teach each other (Col. 3:16).

- *How can we engage with the Bible in a way that every Christian can be involved in?*

....

....

....

We've found that using an interactive Bible discussion method can be one simple way for groups to start engaging with the Bible. All you need to do is choose a Bible passage (perhaps starting with a passage on repentance, faith, baptism or stories from the gospels or Acts) then simply ask three questions:

1. What does this passage mean?
2. What are we going to do in response to it?
3. Who can we share this truth with?

We've found that these questions place the emphasis on obedience rather than head knowledge.

- *What do you think are the non-negotiable beliefs and practices that churches should commit to?*

....

....

....

To guide your discussion, look at the basic practices of the Early Church described in Acts 2:42 and the basic teachings described in Hebrews 6:1-3.

The Basic Practices can be applied simply through Bring+Share. Bring+Share reminds us that church gatherings should be communal, participative, interactive and informal. So we begin with four basic practices from Acts 2:42:

Bring+Share:
- Share Stories (our story and the biblical story)
- Share Life (our whole lives, not just meetings)
- Share Food (meals and the Lord's Supper)
- Share Prayer (our relationship with God)

The Basic Teachings of the Early Church can be applied through Truth+Dare (a concept you're already familiar with). Truth+Dare reminds us that we're committed to acting on truths we hear or read. We don't just intellectually assent to these truths, but we actually dare to do something about them in practical ways. We can apply Truth+Dare to the six basic teachings of Hebrews 6:1-3:

Truth+Dare:
- Repentance
- Faith

- Baptisms
- Laying on of hands
- Resurrection
- Judgement

The basic teaching can be introduced to the Person of Peace and their group through the interactive Bible discussion method. Simply read a story about repentance, faith or baptism, for example, and then ask the questions we looked at earlier.

Truth+Dare

There will no doubt be many things in this practice you've found challenging. We believe, however, that this is the pattern set by Jesus and the Early Church — and it has been effective in our experience, too. So we dare you to try it!

- *How will you continue in your commitment to search and pray for People of Peace?*

  ....
  ....
  ....

- *When you find them, what commitment will you make to regularly disciple them and help them reach their network?*

  ....
  ....
  ....

- *When the time is right, how will you go about encouraging the Person of Peace to draw together a regular group?*

....
....
....

- *Will you commit to Show, Help, Observe then Withdraw from the new simple church, having laid the basic teachings and practices?*

....
....
....

You can move onto the final practice of 'Persecution' whenever you feel ready, as it's relevant at all stages of pioneer mission.

Our Travels

Plant (Pete)

I started to learn about this whole Pioneer Process while living in Nottingham. Once this process started to take shape, I began to train a team of 12 others in the city to pioneer using the same process we're taking you through in this guide.

Several of the people we've trained have found People of Peace and have coached them to gather together their social circles.

One way my wife Marsha does this is to encourage her People of Peace to write down the names of all their friends, family and neighbours and then commit to regularly praying through that list. Marsha then asks how they might gather together some of the people on the list. One Person of Peace gathered about 20 of her family at her Baptism Party. This meant that her family heard the story of her experience of Jesus and experienced simple church life.

Plant (Tim)

I've formed a number of groups over the years, both in my paid outreach worker role and in my own time. These groups have organically formed through friendships and through more formal seeker courses.

On every occasion I've seen a group form, the natural instinct of that group is to stay together as an ongoing Jesus-centred community. They've never instinctively wanted to disband or integrate into another group or into a traditionally structured church. Not knowing what to do next, I tried on a number of occasions to encourage a group to do just this, but it never ended well!

I've since learnt that the best way to treat these new groups is to encourage them to see themselves as churches in their own right that can network with the wider body of believers. This creates a greater sense of ownership and active participation, and consequently leads to more effective discipleship.

Notes, doodles, sketches…

PRACTICE 7: *PERSECUTION*
[Matthew 10:14-20]

PRACTICE 7: PERSECUTION

Pioneer mission is always accompanied by some form of persecution. For this reason, Jesus ended his teaching on pioneer mission by speaking on the subject of persecution.

This last practice will help your group understand why persecution comes and how we can stand firm against the spiritual, human and circumstantial opposition we'll face.

Pray

Jesus again links the Holy Spirit to mission when he says that in times of persecution the Spirit will give us the words to speak (Mt. 10:19-20). This is a further reminder that, to be effective in pioneer mission, we must maintain a close walk with the Spirit.

Ask Jesus to make us more aware of the Spirit's presence among us. Spend time simply waiting and seeing if the Spirit wants to speak to the group, particularly in the area of opposition we've faced or may face in the future. End by thanking Jesus for all he's done through us in terms of pioneer mission. Ask him to strengthen us against any opposition we may face.

Report back

Spend time reporting back to the group about how your pioneer mission experience is going.

- *Have you found a Person of Peace yet?*

....

....

....

- *Are they beginning to reach out to their family and social network?*

  ....
  ....
  ....

- *Do you feel you're moving towards establishing a simple church?*

  ....
  ....
  ....

- *Is it time for you to leave this new community?*

  ....
  ....
  ....

Engage

Ask someone in the group to read Matthew 10:14-20 out loud. Spend some time meditating on these verses.

- *What is Jesus saying to you about persecution?*

  ....
  ....
  ....

Spend time sharing together as a group. You can use some of the following questions if you feel they would be helpful.

- *Have you ever faced spiritual or human persecution as a result of your faith?*

  ....

  ....

  ....

- *In what form did this persecution come?*

  ....

  ....

  ....

- *Did you find the human or spiritual opposition hardest to stand up against?*

  ....

  ....

  ....

- *Has anyone in the group faced persecution since starting this pioneer mission journey?*

  ....

  ....

  ....

- *What form did it take and what was your response?*

....

....

....

- *Have you sensed that you've been among 'wolves'?*

....

....

....

- *Can you relate to Jesus's command to be 'shrewd' but also 'innocent'?*

....

....

....

Practice

Persecution can come at any time in the Pioneer Process. If we're unprepared for this, it can easily knock us off course.

Persecution is to be expected

Although Jesus came with a message of forgiveness and reconciliation, he was sure that this same message would cause hostility and division. Towards the end of his teaching on pioneer mission he said, 'Do not suppose that I have come to bring peace to the earth. I did not come to bring peace, but a sword' (Mt. 10:34).

- *What do you think it is about the message of the coming Kingdom of God that might cause hostility and division?*

....

....

....

The message Jesus brought directly challenged political and religious allegiances (Jn. 18:37; Mt. 23:8-12). It challenges materialism (Lk. 18:22-25), consumerism (Mt. 6:31-32), hedonism (Lk. 15:13-18) and all other philosophies and belief systems (Jn. 14:6). Jesus isn't expecting us to go looking for trouble, but his own life shows us that if we preach the Kingdom of God with honesty then we're almost certainly going to find it!

- *How might spiritual forces try to oppose us?*

....

....

....

Clearly the devil doesn't want us to spread the message of the Kingdom and lead people into a relationship with Jesus, so he'll try a range of strategies to knock us off course. In many parts of the world, he's trying to physically destroy Christians, which was his first strategy with Jesus (Mt. 2:13-16). Where this strategy isn't possible, he'll try to subtly discourage and distract us, which was his next strategy with Jesus (Mt. 4:1-11).

- *When have you felt discouraged and distracted during your time of pioneer mission?*

....

....

....

- *In what forms did these discouragements and distractions take?*

....

....

....

In the parable of the sower (Mt. 13:3-23), Jesus said that people will fall away from his calling firstly due to 'trouble and persecution' (the devil's first strategy). Then secondly, people will fall away due to 'the worries of this life and the deceitfulness of wealth' (the devil's second strategy). Jesus says that those who stand strong in the face of these distractions will produce 'a hundred, sixty or thirty times what was sown', which is the hope of all good pioneer missionaries. Perhaps that's why some of the most fruitful pioneer mission is taking place in poorer countries, where they aren't distracted by the deceitfulness of wealth.

- *What 'worries of this life' have you recently experienced that have distracted you from pioneer mission?*

....

....

....

* *What is deceitful about wealth and how could it cause you to be distracted from pioneer mission?*

....

....

....

Persecution isn't to be feared

We've found that it helps simply knowing that persecution is part of the Pioneer Process. Paul the apostle, for example, wrote to his apostolic trouble-shooter Timothy saying: 'Everyone who wants to live a godly life in Christ Jesus will suffer persecution' (2 Tim 3:12). Knowing that persecution is part of the process we're committed to helps take away its fear.

* *What good have you seen come from persecution?*

....

....

....

When we've faced spiritual opposition, for example, we've been encouraged because we know that if the devil is trying to stop us we must be heading in the right direction!

Jesus goes as far as saying we're 'blessed' when we face hardships and persecution. Tough times can remind us that we'll one day receive a great reward. We can also be comforted knowing we stand in a long line of God's persecuted people (Mt. 5:10-12). God can also use persecution to refine our character (Rm. 5:3). And we can know we're sharing in Jesus's sufferings (Rm. 8:17).

Jesus never promised us a comfortable life — far from it (Mk. 8:34-35). So don't be discouraged when hardship comes, as this is the life we're called to.

Pioneer missionaries are on the frontline of God's advancing Kingdom. And so, as Paul said to Timothy, we must "endure hardship...like a good soldier of Christ Jesus" (1 Tim. 2:3).

Persecution can be overcome

To help us learn how to overcome persecution and hardship, we're going to look at how the Early Church handled opposition in the Book of Acts.

Get into groups of two or three and read the following passages:

- Acts 4
- Acts 5:17-42
- Acts 6:8-15; 7:51-8:8
- Acts 16:16-36

From these passages, answer the following questions and feed your findings back to the group:

- *Why was the Early Church persecuted?*

....

....

....

- *How were they persecuted?*

....

....

....

- *What was their response to the persecution?*

....

....

....

- *What was the result of the persecution?*

....

....

....

In our experience, and from what we can see from these passages, persecution usually comes when we start boldly and publically proclaiming the message of God's Kingdom. People don't mind a private faith, but when we go public people are offended.

The persecution the Early Church faced came in the form of prison, threats, beatings and false witnesses. We know from historical records that all but one of the first apostles died for their faith. Many Christians around the world are daily facing these same forms of persecution. Western Christians are presently spared much of this, but the tide seems to be turning and pressure on Christians is slowly increasing.

The Early Church responded to this persecution in a remarkably positive way. Rather than being deterred, they spoke even more boldly, continuing in their pioneer work. They prayed and praised, rejoiced and where possible even blessed their persecutors. Following Jesus's advice to 'shake the dust off your feet' (Mt. 10:14), the Early Church also knew when it was time to move on to find people who were open to their message (e.g. Acts 13:49-51). In summary, they turned to Jesus and he blessed them and their pioneering work.

As a result of this response, rather than their pioneering work being limited by persecution, the message actually spread, miracles occurred, People of Peace were found and many came to faith!

- *Do these stories from the Early Church change your response to persecution?*

....

....

....

Truth+Dare
The truths of this practice certainly demand a daring response!

- *How will you respond to persecution and hardships?*

....

....

....

- *How will you as a group support each other through persecution and encourage each other to turn to Jesus?*

....

....

....

- *How will you go about 'shaking the dust off your feet' when you and your message are rejected?*

....

....

....

- *Will you commit to continuing in your calling to pioneer mission, regardless of the cost?*

....

....

....

Our Travels

Persecution (Pete)

Ever since I started out in pioneer mission I've encountered persecution! At first this came from what I thought were unlikely sources — namely Christians and, even worse, Christian leaders! Later, I was abandoned by 'friends' who couldn't understand why leaders were speaking out against what I was doing, or just couldn't relate to my pioneering lifestyle.

God, however, used this persecution to grow my character and deepen my relationship with him. This 'desert experience' (which is how I refer to my first 10 years in pioneer mission!) is a process I believe all pioneers need to go through in order to become completely dependent on God. Through this experience I learnt to go to God in prayer and to read the Bible for myself. That's when I discovered that the things God was leading me to do through pioneer mission weren't so strange after all, it was right there in the Bible!

I've learnt that persecution when combined with obedience and dependence on Jesus can lead to massive spiritual growth! So now I'm actually thankful for the persecution I've experienced as it's helped to keep me humble and reliant on Jesus.

Persecution (Tim)

I've experienced a couple of occasions of spiritual persecution as I've gone about pioneer mission in the area where I currently live. The first was when I delivered the message I believed God had given me for the assistant in the New Age shop.

As I cycled up to the shop, a car pulled up directly in front of me and the driver launched a tirade of verbal abuse. I asked him what I'd done, but he just carried on shouting and shaking his fist. I soon sensed that this was a tactic of the enemy to try and stop me going into the shop (and it almost worked, as I was pretty shaken up by it). Once I realised this, I prayed for God's protection and walked into the shop, and the car drove off.

Notes, doodles, sketches…

WHERE TO NEXT?

Well done! You've now journeyed with us through the 7 Practices! However, that doesn't signal the end of your pioneering journey…far from it. God is calling us to a life of pioneer mission.

So we'd encourage you not to view the 7 Practices simply as a linear sequence. This journey isn't as straightforward as seven stops on a bus route.

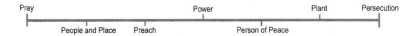

Jesus did teach these practices one after the other, and they do serve as a helpful pattern to follow. This journey, however, doesn't have a definite end point that is reached after we've progressed through the 7 Practices. It's also important to remember that all of these practices can intersect each other at any point. We've both, for example, experienced persecution when only just starting out on the first practice.

Neither would we encourage a purely cyclical view of these practices. Following the 7 Practices isn't the same as travelling on a circular bus route.

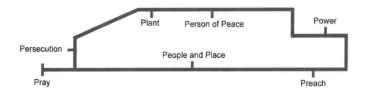

Although this view helpfully shows that the journey (i.e. each practice and the entire process) doesn't have a clear end point, it unhelpfully suggests that the practices occur in a purely linear sequence.

Instead, we'd encourage you to view the 7 Practices as an entire bus route map.

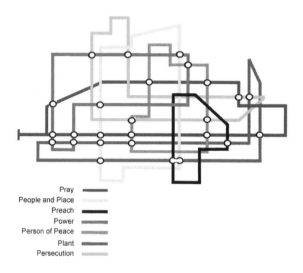

Pray	▬▬▬
People and Place	▬▬▬
Preach	▬▬▬
Power	▬▬▬
Person of Peace	▬▬▬
Plant	▬▬▬
Persecution	▬▬▬

Rather than the practices being stops on this map, each practice is an individual circular bus route. This shows that each practice continues throughout the process and that any of the practices can intersect at different points during the process. So we're always praying, always open to the possibility we'll be led to new people and places, and we always take opportunities to preach and demonstrate the Kingdom in power. We're always looking for People of Peace who will gather their network to form a church and we're always aware that persecution might come at any time.

The Pioneer Process is a continual journey. It's a mindset, a way of life. It's not a formula that will guarantee instant results. Rather, it's a set of practices that with commitment and patience will slowly begin to advance God's Kingdom among the people and places he has called you to.

So keep praying and keep referring back to Matthew 10 and Luke 10 in order to stay in touch with your travel guide, Jesus.

We hope that you enjoy the journey and that through it God is glorified.

ANY FUTURE TRAVEL PLANS?

If *Pioneer Mission* has whetted your appetite for more travel then look out for the forthcoming publications from *Newforms*:

Simple Church

This guide follows on from *Pioneer Mission* and is for those who are looking for more detailed guidance in forming blessed, fruitful, multiplying churches.

The guide will wrestle with a wide range of questions relating to simple organic church, including:

- *What is Church?*
- *What do we do when we meet together?*
- *How can we form open, participatory, Spirit-led meetings?*
- *How can we reach out to others?*
- *How can we multiply churches?*

Making Disciples

This guide also follows on from *Pioneer Mission* and goes into greater detail about the disciple-making process.

The guide will tackle such questions as:

- *What does it mean to be a disciple of Jesus?*
- *What do we do someone when comes to faith in Jesus?*
- *How can we train them to make disciples themselves?*
- *What do we do when people give up?*
- *How do we make disciples who make disciples?*

Pioneer Series

Also look out for future publications in the *Pioneer Series*, including *Pioneer Prayer* and *Pioneer Evangelism*.

STILL WANT MORE?

Training
Pioneer Mission, *Simple Church* and *Making Disciples* are all delivered as training systems. These can take place over a weekend, 3 consecutive days or through a 4-session course over a period of 4 weeks (each session lasting 2-3 hours). Go to the Newforms website for more details.

Regional Days
We can help you facilitate gatherings in any of the 12 regions of Britain. These days involve networking and equipping simple organic missional churches and those interested in knowing more about the movement.

UK Gatherings
Each year we host the UK's national simple/missional church gathering. These gatherings bring together simple and missional communities from across the country and equip them through the ministry of leading thinkers and practitioners from around the world.

Websites
missionbritain.com
This site acts as a resource and networking hub for pioneers, trainers and mission strategy coordinators across the nation.

simplechurch.co.uk
This site acts as a resource and networking hub for those involved in simple organic expressions of church.

simplestories.co.uk
This site shares inspiring and informative stories of people following the Pioneer Process across the country.

newformsresources.com

This site is the home of all the audio, visual and written resources produced by *Newforms*. It's also the place to go to book training and experiences.

Notes, doodles, sketches…